MOLLUSC

Mark Totterdell was born and brought up in rural Somerset and now lives in Exeter, where he works as a copywriter. His early enthusiasm for poetry was tempered by studying literature to degree level, and it was only in middle age that he began writing again seriously. Since then, his poems have appeared widely in magazines and anthologies and he has achieved success in many competitions. This is his third collection.

By the same author

This Patter of Traces
(Oversteps Books, 2014)

Mapping
(Indigo Dreams Publishing, 2018)

MOLLUSC

Mark Totterdell

The High Window

First published in the UK in 2021 by The High Window Press
3 Grovely Close
Peatmoor
Swindon
SN5 5DN
Email: abbeygatebooks@yahoo.co.uk

The right of Mark Totterdell to be identified as the author of this work has been asserted by him in accordance with Copyright, Designs and Patent Act, 1988. © Mark Totterdell 2021
ISBN: 9798519896344

All rights reserved. No part of this book may be reproduced or transmitted in any form or by any means, electronic or mechanical, including photocopying, recording, or by any information storage and retrieval system, without permission in writing from the copyright owner. This book may not be lent, hired out, resold or otherwise disposed of by way of trade in any form of binding or cover other than that in which it is published, without prior consent of the publishers.

Designed and typeset in Palatino Linotype by The High Window Press.
Front Cover Photograph: © Jane Thomas 2021
Printed and bound by kdp.amazon.com

CONTENTS

INSECTS

The Aurelians   10
Jersey Tiger Moth   11
Lampyris   12
Gerris   13
Colias   14
Geotrupes   15
Dasychira   16
Argynnis   17
Pieris   18
Blaps   19
Apatele   20
Chorthippus   21
Eyed Hawk Moth   22

BIRDS

Choughs   24
Choughed   25
The Choughs on the Cliff   26
Long-tailed Tits   27
House Sparrows   28
Blue Tit   29
Turnstones   30
The Blackbird's Plumage   31
Allotment Pheasant   32
Redwing   33

The Parrot and the Dove   34
Egret   35
Mistle   36
Teal   37
Old Sludge Beds   38
Nestling   39
House Martins   40
Treecreeper   41
The Ravens in the Library   42
Dipper   44

THIS

Alpaca   46
Amber Dagger Pommel   47
Andromeda   48
Bufo   49
Capreolus   50
Carcinus   51
Clod   52
Fabiform   53
Fin Whale   54
First Great Western   55
Form   56
Frog   57
Ghost   58
Heath   59
Hirudo   60
Hiss   61
It   62

Jack   63
Leaf   64
Mary   65
Nether Exe   66
One Night I Slept on Land that Isn't There   67
On the Trail of STC   68
Playtime   70
Purse   72
Realm   73
Rhinoceros   74
Right of Way, West Penwith   75
Rough   76
Snowdrops   77
Solomon's Hollow   78
Solstice   79
Spawn   81
Stars   82
Tachyglossus   83
Temple Meads   84
The Badger   85
This   86
Two Leaves   87
Wormcasts   88

MOLLUSCS

Dissolve   90
Malacophagy   91
The Slug and the Puffball   92
Slugs   93
Helix   94
Snails   95

Cepaea 96
Snail 97
Polymath 98
Shell 99
Light 100
Mytilus 101
Holdfast 102
Nacre 103
Ming 104
Janthina 105
Ammonites 106
Belemnites 107
Cameroceras 108
Nautilus 109
Argonaut 110
Benthic 111
Suckers 112
Escapologist 113
Pseudomorph 114
Aliens 115
Octopus 116

INSECTS

The Aurelians

Foppish, they'd stride the wild unhindered heath,
flapping great nets in homage to their quarry,
then, in a loving spirit of enquiry,
shut golden fluttering wings in jars of death;

alien to us. We let those creatures live
we smile to find on fragments that remain.
Bad air accumulates; we might bemoan
the ways we've come to kill the things we love.

Jersey Tiger Moth

It's settled boldly on our white front door,
an emblem with the look of something rare;
soft arrowhead in simple origami,
printed with patterns not quite black and white,
but pale vanilla, bitter chocolate,
in glam rock zigzags, like a dazzle ship.
It flies, and its flashed underskirts are gaudy,
the perfect shade of tinned tomato soup.

Their home is Portugal, is Greece, is Russia.
There's one famed island valley where they swarm.
It's only natural for them to come
into this land of high unnatural pressure.
Their shtick is to bear whole wide bright worlds here,
enrich thin lives, exoticise plain air.

Lampyris

Lower your eyes from the stars. They seem too faint
to count for much, too distant to be true.
Among the grass at your feet are tiny beings,
bearing soft dots of living luminescence,
pale greenish glow of radium, or deep glint
of emerald, as beetle signals beetle.
In the small complex wonders of their bodies,
luciferin combines with oxygen
to form their nightshines, bright gleams with no heat,
a golden constellation in the darkness,
with you alone to witness it tonight.

Gerris

The skim of the skater
on skin of flat water,
its legs a thin saltire;
each foot makes a dimple
sufficient to alter
the light on the surface,
a shadow-distorter,
so on the mud under
the pool of clear water,
the shadow of skater
is graced with an aura
at every quarter.

Colias

Yolk among egg white,
gem among stones,
spark among papers,
soul among bones,
gold among silver,
hymn among tunes,
flame among ashes,
sun among moons.

Geotrupes

There's been an event, here on the forest track.
A mass of stuff has dropped. Already a force
of small beings has fuzzed its domed surfaces,
while others dance, particles round a nucleus.

Here comes the dirt-borer, the true old dumbledor,
the lousy watchman, crawling like clockwork
on carbon fibre legs. Its back is a grooved shield,
its sheen a rainbow of indigo and black.

It comes in at an angle, then it hits
but doesn't stop; asteroid striking planet,
slow bullet through flesh. It plunges its dark self
deeper and deeper into soft succulent shit.

Dasychira

It's a bright confection,
on the cusp of yellow and pale green,
fizzing with filaments,
bristling with toothbrushy tussocks,
the tuft on its rump
dipped in crimson ink.

Then it curls
into a plump comma,
flashes its velvety gussets
of utter,
utter
black.

Argynnis

Pearl-bordered –
patches of brightness embossed on the dark.

Dark Green –
dew still on undergrowth when the sun's high.

High Brown –
burgundy edgings to half-moons of silver.

Silver-washed –
underwing abstract of mother-of-pearl.

Pieris

One term, a constant crawl,
yellowy-green and black,
streamed from the cabbage patch;
moored on the school's high wall.

Next, each brought forth its few
odd blobs of fuzzy yellow.
Kids said 'they're caterpillar
eggs'. Even then I knew

smaller grubs had consumed
these large ones from inside,
emptied them out alive,
hollowed them, left them doomed

not to pupate. None would
ever emerge, unfurl
fine sets of full white sails,
launch into adulthood.

Blaps

Blaps. Blaps.
Blaps.
Six thin feet pacing
to the slow click
of an antique clock.
It's so late,
here in this dim cellar,
or old churchyard,
or under these
nailed-down floorboards.
The sharp end of its body,
the dull black of its back,
as if it's dressed
for dark formality;
the whiff of it, as if
it's past its point of no return;
its stiff-legged course
towards the furthest corner.
Blaps mucronata. Blaps mucronata.
Blaps
mu cro na ta…

Apatele

Its lower flanks are pale, matt metal-grey,
with just a hint of porthole in black dots.
Above, you have to love the subtle way
grey stipples into black; those blood-red spots.
Then, to complete its bold, wild colour scheme,
the dorsal stripe's what you could call rich cream
or palest yellow. Though, like me and you,
beneath the skin it's all just guts and goo.

Chorthippus

thippus
thippusthippus
thippusthippusthippuschor
thippuschorthippuschorthippus

assgr
assgrassgr
assgrassgrassgrassgr
assgrassgrassgrassgrasshopper

Eyed Hawk Moth

Seeking some hope this week
in grass beneath the apple tree,
I find its body, downside-up,
a dull and lifeless symmetry.

I turn it. Bark-brown forewings
half hide, in this stiff pose,
the shocking bright blue rings
of untrue eyes, set against rose;

a frail perfection of loose-fixed scales,
a triumph of undesign.
Hopeful beyond reason, I rest it
on a branch, witness a sign,

the faintest quiver in its wings,
a minor, vital resurrection.
It's only a trick of the wind,
and even the trick's a fiction.

BIRDS

Choughs

The sea today is all
white roar and roll.
Two finger-feathered choughs
ping off split granite.
Their return
is like a miracle,
an unlikely story
of early Celtic saints.
They're pure black,
but for beaks and feet
the tempting cherry-red
of nail varnish, lipstick.

Choughed

Thrift and soft grasses have made me a mattress
beneath the high overhang's dark rocky buttress.

Two choughs are feeding, each crimson bill probing,
describing an arc round its centre of being.

Each has been bound with a band of bright plastic
to keep them from floating off out to the mystic.

'This pair' said the birder 'are brother and sister',
tut-tutting his fear of genetic disaster.

No bird is blacker, but when they fly over
the cliffs in late sunlight, they turn a pure silver.

The Choughs on the Cliff

A cry like a 'ciao'.
For less than a minute,
we watch birds who wear
the black of a widow.

One goes into air,
one stays on pale granite.
One's feather and bone,
the other's all shadow.

Long-tailed Tits

A grid of names and greyness
has been laid on this land.
In great blank boxes
in Bittern Road and Kestrel Way,
stuff is being made or moved
for money.

Among small pockets of the past,
in old oaks where hedges were,
a band of small adventurers
are pecking a scant living,
somehow, anyhow, from twigs,
keeping in contact
with soft, thin calls,
before launching themselves
over tarmac oceans
to the next unnamed green island.

House Sparrows

Where did the sparrows dwell
before we built spaces
by chance for them
in the chinks of our houses
and homed those tiny spirits
of our safe places?

How did the sparrows fare,
what did they feast upon,
before they took their tithes of tithes
of our stored corn?
How will the sparrows fend
once we are gone?

Blue Tit

Crown and wings blue,
the too-true blue
at the zenith of a cloudless sky.

Breast yellow,
the green-tinged shade
of a young leaf unfolding.

Face white, dark-marked,
like a comedy mask
strapped to the head.

(the angry grey-blue of
a thundercloud ready to burst.)

(shade of an old leaf fading,
draining of green before its fall.)

(like the imagined skull
close under feather and paper-thin skin.)

Turnstones

On the stony beach below
this artists' town of granite,
slate and deep yellow lichen,

they forage, invisible,
their backs an abstract
of bladderwrack and bedrock,

then fly, flash black and white,
soft pencil marks on paper.
They spill up to the quay,

risk tourists' feet, compete
for scraps with the pirate gulls,
but meekly, meekly.

There was the tale of the pair
who took the ferry every day,
avian trippers tamed with names,

but truer by far is the pull
of the north in their frail skulls,
their flight over earth's vast curve.

The Blackbird's Plumage

is armour,
each plate beaten thin
for the brave dark knight of the dawn,

is aura
made visible, soft surround
of the skinny bony thing within,

is emblem,
a charge of pure sable
on a field of vert,

is engine,
interlock of remiges,
of rectrices. Uplift. Flight.

Allotment Pheasant

Forager for winter greens,
cock of the plot, with a strut
and a swagger that say
he's bang up to date with the rent.

Fool in a three-colour cap, performing
his knockabout greenhouse routine,
attempting a comedy exit –
thud, thud – through a hard clear pane.

Refugee from the killing fields
out of town, where the shot drops like rain,
where he's classed by every paying gun
as fine fair game.

Warrior with no comrades,
in subtle armour wrought by no hands,
his precious breast guarded
by a thousand discs of bronze.

Redwing

There's just one, flockless and unshy, in a tree
on the industrial estate. The pale
supercilium. The tell-tale flash on the flank
like a splash of sustaining rowanberry.

It slipped south, tseeping unseen by night
through porous borders, down before the snow,
stirring images, or memories, of tundra,
unlikely vastnesses away and ago;

the wonder of someone, some me, to have witnessed
that ideal nest set low in stunted willow.

The Parrot and the Dove

Inside, beyond the pane, behind the bars,
he's in his tight suit of matt-grey chain-mail,
clacking the keyless padlock of his beak,
flaring his crimson molten-metal tail.

She flutters unfettered across an open sky.
Her black velvet collar is undone. Her scale,
her shape, her shade, suggest she's his far sister,
set up the parallel, the glib freedom-fable.

But what if the tiny birdcage of her self
is utter, inescapable constraint?
What if his dark eyes easily encompass
a world unwalled, unroofed and infinite?

Egret

Paint-white, it puts the oily swans to shame.
It's poddering dead leaves in submerged mud,
the yellow comedy rubber chicken feet
pounding up and down beneath twin black shafts.

A small crowd have gathered at the river's edge.
It fans out wings with ballerina elegance,
and now it darts, jabs hard with a wrought-iron poker.
Its eye, to my eye, holds something like wisdom.

I want to leave it there. It almost stumbles
over a lump of expanded polystyrene,
sidesteps bottles of crumpled polyethylene,
still keeping, to my mind, something like dignity.

Mistle

The day the sky grew dull as lead,
as the old year was set to die,
I heard its distant hard bright voice,
a message that got no reply,

more urgent than the blackbird's song,
in what seemed like a minor key,
one phrase repeated, unresolved,
a never-finished melody.

I sought and found it far and high,
a mere dot in a tree, from where
I couldn't see its bold streaked breast,
grey back, beak scissoring cold air,

and still its loud and keen laments
got no reply, as if it were
unmatched, unrivalled, all alone,
the only bird of Devonshire.

Teal

A brace of teal shoot up from the ruffled river
at our approach. They're little more than half-ducks.
What would she do if he flew off with another?

She is the subtle one, in her coat of cryptics,
an earthscape of dead leaves and twigs in every feather.
How would he ever live if she fell to the fox?

He is the dandy, in chestnut and emerald headwear,
his back fine-lined with a thousand whites and blacks.
What would he do if she flew off with another?

Matching green bands show brightly as each wing flicks,
caught in the late sun as they fly together.
How would she ever live if he fell to the fox?

Old Sludge Beds

The former sewage settlement lagoons,
a wasteland wedged between the river's curves
and an elbow of equivalent canal,
have been recolonised by sedges,
by bulrushes releasing feathered seeds,
by tall blond reeds in broad stands, rustling
with unseen life, suspicious scurryings.

From leafless trees, the great tits and song thrushes
are cleanly piping out, respectively,
their simple and their complex repetitions.
Close your eyes and you can almost see
the sounds as clear distinctive prints
cutting into the greyish sludge that spreads
everywhere from the traffic on the bridge.

Nestling

Among the grass of our safe childhood garden,
we found a tiny monster, which had fallen,
ugly as sin, from somewhere in the skies.
We gaped at its impossible, pink foulness,
a shocking, insupportable near-foetus,
with dull blue bruises where it wanted eyes,

and as we stared in unbelieving wonder,
it forced our eyes to open ever wider,
and climbed into our minds, where it took hold.
Thus were we dispossessed of our snug haven,
thrown to the wicked world, our nest unwoven,
our new horizons vast and grim and cold.

House Martins

Where the winter river dumped its load
of mud onto the flood relief channel's
concrete, there's one corner of the stuff that's not
too sloppy now, or crazy-paving cracked yet.

Here there are birds out of air, briefly grounded,
filling thin bills more used to spindly insects,
then streaming in loose flocks beyond the trees
to where it's necessary to imagine

all their fine affixings of gobbets of cob
to stone, to brick, to the undersides
of painted wooden eaves, defying the drop;
the martins joining their houses to ours.

Treecreeper

It's the shape of a leaf;
its bill and tail
are apex and petiole.

It's the shades of cracked bark,
split with the palest
cream of heartwood.

It's a satellite
orbiting its world
of greynesses, green moss.

It's here. It's here. It's here.
Jink, jink, jink, as if in
a one-frame-per-second film.

It's tracing a neat helix
upwards around the trunk.
It's gone.

The Ravens in the Library

One day, the ravens forsook their moor,
left squishy lambs' eyes and spaghetti guts,
and aimed and fired themselves at the heart of the city.

First they put on a fine black arrow display
upside-downside-up above the flat roof
of the cheaply refurbished central library,

then they dropped anchors to our level,
where their dark dense matter triggered the wheeze
of the automatic doors, and they were in,

a havoc, scattering the clients of the café,
piercing the fading ghosts of redundant librarians,
their kronk-kronks ricocheting off bare walls.

They flew dead straight to the flimsy shelving,
began to peck and tear at all the books,
got high on the glue of the bindings.

They ripped the innards out, they tore and swallowed
chunks of encyclopaedia, a Collected Poems
and more, eating paper, ink and all, as if

thereby they'd somehow absorb the sense, the meanings,
become human-wise. As if this is a fable.
As if there's more to be read into it.

Their acids did their work, and in an hour
the tacky carpet tiles were constellated
with stinks of their soft, blank, papier-mâché shit.

Dipper

A silver coin of sunlight pinging off the stiff
small wave where the black river meets a riffle,

a pure stain of long-grown lichen, the shining
city on its small brown hill of river stone,

a pale umbel of dropwort, its stalk angling it over
so it softly nods at the shadowed edge of the river,

a full moon of spinning moor foam in slow orbit,
eddying round the river's pool of night,

and only then the creamy breast set against deepest
peat-dark river shades. Only then the dipper.

THIS

Alpaca

She's the pick of the skittish flock, with the frizz
of her oversize pale coat, her snub cartoon
muzzle. He could orbit perpetually
the dark new worlds of her eyes.

He plunges a finger, three knuckles deep,
into the soft dense fibres at her nape.
She stays and utters, not quite a bleat,
the lips unparted, but something like a hum

for him to make a meaning from.
He hopes it's a murmur of pleasure,
though he'd plump for mere acceptance.
He's sure it's not pure frozen terror.

Amber Dagger Pommel

There was a tree that shed a tear of flame
which dropped onto the earth, where it set hard.

There was a hand that shaped it like an eye
and pierced it with a hundred points of gold

and made of it, with wooden hilt and blade
of bronze, a thing fit for some lord of war.

There was a mound of earth, bone-ash and stone
where it lay long unseen, unthought-of, cold.

There was a mind that sought, and delved, and found,
and set it proudly in a case of glass.

There was a fire that fell out of the sky
and blitzed it back into cold earth again.

Andromeda

How bright we are
to see the fixed stars and the falling star
and grasp their simple size and distance ratio,
to know
that one's a local speck,
those others massive,
unimaginably far.

It has to be,
extending this geometry,
one fuzzy star
is a whole multi-billion star galaxy,
a smudge that's vaster, magnitudes more far
than all besides that we,
with our faint eyes,
will ever see.

Bufo

Can it be glad I picked it off the path?
It's dull as mud, gnarled as a crumpled leaf.

It squats in my hand, unmetaphorical.
Is this walled scrap of garden all its world?

Its warts will not be charmed or doctored off.
There is no gem, but is the poison real?

And is it true what I knew as a child?
Does my skin burn its cool skin like a flame?

Capreolus

Even the water's walled here;
whole wooded miles
tamed by the dams and channels
of old stone mills.

Glimpsed through the trees, in water;
a great brown hound?
No. Something older, wilder,
split-footed, horned,

runs past the oaks and ashes,
then clears the sharp
wire that's the world's far margin
for fieldbound sheep.

Carcinus

The beach is a zillion sandgrains,
galaxy-wide.
At the top, where the cliffs might tumble down,
there's trash and treasure dumped by the tide;

this perfect-sculpted brittle carapace,
those countless plastic scraps
that a man grabs with a plastic litter-picker
to put in plastic sacks,

Sisyphus in a high-vis jacket.
What can I do but wish him well,
though he might as well try to bail out the sea
with scoop after scoop of this crabshell.

Clod

Rolling away the clod reveals
a trinity of newts, curled like commas,
tiny heraldic beasts,
rhymes for the pale dead roots around them.

Last year, I chucked this hunk of earth
and made, by chance, their thin winter world.

May I set this against
my felling of the frogs' safe groves of grass,
each careless wormchop, each act
of blue murder on the simple slugs?

Fabiform

is the name for that shape, the oval profile
slightly indented on the side with the navel.

All summer there's been subtle vegetable sex,
combining, recombining. It's like rolling

dice now, thumbing open the husks;
the black ones, the white ones, fit for counters

in board games, or these standard pinks, marbled
with a mauve that fades when boiled,

that look like stuff inside you, reminding you
that once upon a time, *meat* meant any food.

Fin Whale

News travels quickly through this medium.
You need to see it so you can say you saw it.
Half an hour later you're bombing down the ring road.

From half a mile away, up on the cliff top,
it's greyish, sluglike, a smudge against the sand.
The swarm of midges round it must be people.

Close up, you join an ambling congregation.
You orbit the great dead planet of the body,
its ridges and valleys, the craters and erosion.

You want to touch it so you can say you touched it.
The baleen is made of thick black plastic plates,
components of a machine that you can't work.

Its eye is tiny, piggy. Your nose is open
to molecules of decay. There are officials.
It's a massive headache for the local council.

First Great Western

There are games you can play
when the night's outside.
You can watch the window people,
then turn to match them to their solid selves
as they lurch along the aisle.
The likenesses are sometimes quite uncanny.

And if you didn't know, you wouldn't know
this half-a-minute pressure in your ears
marked the tunnel though the hill
that severs Somerset and Devon;
here and there, house and home, now and then.

And with no clues at all from all that dark,
it's easy to pretend
that, instead of moving forwards,
you are really hurtling back.

Form

Our field where the grasses grew high, won't you look,
has grown a hard harvest of tarmac and brick,
a new human haven that went up too quick
on the sweet tangled wildness where, going way back,

we found the small hare in the warmth of its form,
a shivering thing we'd have hated to harm
that, with young green concern, we proceeded to damn
when we scooped it from safety and carried it home.

Frog

Let's say that it sports the long hooped shorts
of an Edwardian athlete setting a jumping record,

let's say that it's in khaki, khaki combat fatigues,
belly-crawling under the bramble's razor wire,

let's say that it dwells with silent dignity among
the stench and fester of the compost slum,

let's say that it sprang into life, fully-formed,
from the scraps of guilty plastic that it lurks beneath,

let's say that the golden orbs of its eyes
see just what's what. And it's not saying.

Ghost

'Goodnight!' They kill his light and go downstairs.
He can see nothing, but doesn't want to see.
In this old house, he can just hear their chatter,
muffled, although he's in a distant realm.
Armed with his incantation to ward off
the sight he dreads, armed with his affirmation
to back it up, armed with a child's perverse
conviction that, whatever words he utters,
the opposite will happen, he lies awake
for endless minutes in the creaking dark.
'I *will* see a ghost!' he chants, and 'It *won't* work!'

Heath

This lizard could be last year's lizard's son,
that lark may sing the song his father sang,
but here, it seems each spring is every spring,
the same green season since the heath began,
and in this moment, I'm forever young,
the world is going well, and you're not gone.

Hirudo

We fished it from the canal and fetched it home.
Delighted, we gave it a childish, chiming name.
We feared no harm from it, meant it no harm.

We installed it in my room, in a goldfish bowl.
It seemed to settle, as far as we could tell.
It sat like a still black tongue in its clear glass bell,

then shifted from pulsing blob to waving dark
trunk, then kept on performing its nifty trick
of morphing from dash to fat dot, from ball to dick.

I was so happy to keep it by my bed
and watch it, with not a thought in my soft green head
that my pet might pierce my skin and slurp my blood.

I slept, and in the morning it had gone,
as if some tiny miracle had been done,
or sleight of hand. We never saw it again,

but kept for many weeks to come a dread
of treading on its body, shrivelled, dried,
or, far worse, grossly swollen and undead.

Hiss

This year's first snake I heard before I saw.
I was on the heath, lifting sheets of metal
with some hope of success, but also hoping
to fail. It seemed like cheating. What I sought
were snakes out in the open. A short burst
of static somewhere close, and there it was,
in heather, a feisty male, bright black and grey
with cinder eyes. I listened to its crossness,
the suck and the exhale. Its body swelled
and shrank each time, and then it lunged an inch
or two. I'd given it a yard, but still
my heart thumped. Then I left it, heard the hiss
of rain on last year's desiccated grass.

It

It was glimpsed for half a second in the headlights,
stretch-necked and lolloping towards the loch,
with a lamb or something dangling,

it was shot on grainy film, blown up
to a big figure footing it through trees,
unarguable but for japes and ape suits,

it ravaged the village with flame, on unlikely wings,
was slain by a local hero with a lance
that is still on show in the church, but not this church,

it left a ripped-out carcass on the moor,
and one ambiguous paw-print in coarse granite sand,
a blur on a photo where the scale's not clear,

it peered through a midwest midnight window,
huge black almond eyes in a cartoon face,
in a time of odd lights and alleged mutilations,

it pads beside you, claws clicking on tarmac,
then turns to suck the marrow from your spine,
lick your brainpan clean of serotonin.

Jack

I stuck on the beanpoles
last year's carved pumpkin,
half meaning to scare
the birds, or something.

Half a year after,
and Jack is no more.
He's one with the earth,
he's nowhere, everywhere.

All that's left is
this tough peduncle,
this fibrous stalk,
this odd umbilicus.

Where stalk stuck to fruit,
there's a hard hard scar,
between bulging pentagon
and blunted five-point star.

Leaf

Obeying its dynamics, one leaf falls,
more side-to-side than down, in front of me.

A memory; *each leaf you catch, you earn
one day of good luck in the coming year.*

Instinctively, my right hand snatches, misses,
my left hand snaps, grabs it the second go.

It's like a paper heart, the palest yellow
except for constellations of black dots.

Some kind of mould? Pollution? I can't say,
but slip it in my pocket anyway.

Mary

At the end of the green damp lane out of the village,
in the rounded head of a cross, there's a granite man,
carved in saint-patient days. There's a bright sharp
crystal at his heart. Slow centuries of lichen
have piebalded him. Across the fields, brown cows
are mourning as if their god had died. I'm primed
now for images. A worn grey saw-stub,
a lump at the base of the trunk of a tall pine,
leaps out to my unfaithed eye as a faultless Mary.

Nether Exe

...there is no track
to the small church that squats by trees.
You cut through fields of yielding blades,
past badger setts like opened graves.
That rabbit – sent to be your guide? –
is veering madly, myxie-eyed.
The few new headstones, alien slates,
are chiselled deep with names, with dates,
but flocks of fieldfares *chack-a-chack*
with urgent arctic auguries.
You near the porch. Each basalt block
is pocked with holes like emptied eyes.
You reach the door, then realise
you lack the key that turns this lock...

One Night I Slept on Land that Isn't There

One night I slept on land that isn't there,
the cliff now tumbled to the beach below.
So much that once was firm has turned to air.

I was so cocksure then, so free from care,
I had no better place to sleep, and so
one night I slept on land that isn't there.

The music carried on, sweet, wild and rare.
I heard it float up from the town's bright glow.
So much that once was firm has turned to air.

The warm turf cushioned me, the stars were fair.
Why should it matter now that you should know
one night I slept on land that isn't there?

And when the early sun caressed my hair,
I knew for certain which way I should go.
So much that once was firm has turned to air.

My maps are ashes now, so who knows where
the paths went? I'm impelled to tell you, though,
one night I slept on land that isn't there,
so much that once was firm has turned to air.

On the Trail of STC

In Ottery, where Coleridge was born
in a house now shrunk to a photo and a plaque,
a rill whispers its flimsy anecdote

of paper boats, and in the painted ribcage
of the church, I fail to take in much
beyond sun, moon and stars on an ancient clock.

Silver Street, Gold Street. There are twists to this town,
so I keep crossing on blind corners. A placard
reads 'Officer sorry for running man over.'

The brightest thing beneath a lifeless sky
is the signage on the pine-clad supermarket.
A helicopter circles inexplicably.

In Tourist Information; '*Kubla Khan*...'
(with a sneer of disapproval?) '...was the *Lucy
in the Sky with Diamonds* of its day.'

Jesu Street, Mill Street. Down at Tumbling Weir,
beside the crumbling brickwork of the factory,
waters cascade into a manmade cavern.

Measureless saplings, sheathed in plastic, line
the tarmac to the eponymous new bridge
over his original sacred river.

The leaflet promises 'Poetry Stones' in the Land
of Canaan, but the words fail to conjure
them up, the vision has outrun the fact.

'He left the town when he was eight, you know.'
They're waiting to be shipped over. I imagine them
lying in a warehouse way beyond Shangdu.

Playtime

When I was six, one morning playtime,
I looked at the playground climbing frame,

a scary construction of metal tubes,
flakily painted in high-sky blue.

I watched all the big boys monkeying
right up to the top. Then, without thinking,

I jumped and grabbed at the lowest bar.
My small hands slipped, I was grasping air,

I fell for ever…until I landed
flat on the hard ground, dazed and winded.

Then kind Joanna, who had my heart,
sneaked us into the infants' hut.

With kids' blunt scissors, she helped me cut
from an old magazine a cartoon cat.

That patch of old school knee-scrape tarmac
has long been turned to rose-filled garden,

my primary girl, the kind Joanna,
for all I know is now someone's grandma,

but that paper cat, with its purry smile
and its orange stripes, is with me still.

Purse

Lurking among the foam and the black
bladderwrack along the top of the tide,
it's an odd oblong, this horn-cornered purse,
a curved keeled thing in shiny kelp-brown

with a faux-leather look, plasticky almost,
no sign of a button, a hook or a clasp
where it might fix shut, no kind of a clue
to whether it has cleared itself out or not

already of its small quick silver change,
so let us offer it one last thin chance
and chuck it back into the churning surf.
And watch the callous sea chuck it straight back.

Realm

From an upstairs window here at home,
the double line of ragged hills looks flat
as file dividers in slightly different tones
of blue. The thrill of finding a wide realm
between them! Old farms with undead yellow elms,
immense bronze globes of oaks, silver power lines,
field beyond field like undiscovered rooms
in semi-lucid dreams, the shaggy grasslands
where owls bomb down on voles. Among maize haulms,
a stone like a misformed egg has cracked wide open
where the plough has caught it, and there's a whole
tiny intricate crystal world within it.
It's time to draw back and close the cabinet.

Rhinoceros

Ridiculous, inverted, each leg strapped,
its grey bulk swings beneath the helicopter.
It's out cold. The curved horn points groundwards
as it flies higher, an unwilling Icarus.

It's lowered gently, infinitely gently,
into the wilderness that is its promised land.
That horn is drilled, quite painlessly, to take
the high-tech electronic tracking kit.

It wakes alone, unknowingly unwilded.
You raise a three-quarter-hearted cheer
to this mad plan to make amends
to something precious. This preposterousness.

Right of Way, West Penwith

Green dashes, thin black lines. There is no symbol
for nettles piercing cotton cloth to skin,

for tiny spiders setting unseen snares
to catch my flinching face in steely silk,

for how the blocky granite of old stiles
has been clad in lichens (earthstain, adderskin

and eggyolk), or how any absent steps
have been botched new with concrete, or rusty bars.

A map is useful, to bat away the brambles
that, left and right, shoot in to slow my way.

On quite another scale, a fat white ship
is slugging its way across the sea's green leaf.

Rough

Your bed's a king-size square of too-thin card,
and in your dreams it makes the ground less hard.
Your lumpy duvet slips and will not stay,
a cover of thick cloud that's blown away.
The sun's your final coin to feed the meter.
You can't control the setting of the heater.
The moon's your bedside lamp. Just watch it wane.
Your power supply is on the blink again.
Your roof needs fixing. In it, shining bright,
are several thousand tiny holes of light.
Your windows are of air. Their zero-glazing
is 0% efficient. It's amazing.
Your front door is the gap between two trees,
and all the world has access to the keys.

Snowdrops

Among the hedgerow banks that flank Gant's Lane,
you find their clusters coming into bud
through dark soil, dropped leaves, under stark grey
    trees.
You know their beauty, though they cannot please
when you're so cut off, when your mood is mud.

His hair grew snowdrop-white, his mind began
to lose its hold on names. Those galaxies
of small white stars, what were they called again?
The words dropped one by one out of his brain.

Breast feathers from a swan, fine slips of silk,
thin curls of paper, splashes of cold milk,
a close-up snowscape starting to melt green.
Just underground, the busy bulb, unseen,
distils hope drop by drop. Galantamine.

Solomon's Hollow

was what we called it, where the thin road dipped
and rose – was it named on any map? – and a field
or two away, hidden among tall trees
that swayed and sighed, was the cut of the dead canal
where it entered the hill, its gape lipped by stone –
or was it brick? – and fitted with a grille
only a bat could navigate. In the black shallows
one time, a grass snake was all anaconda,

and once we went badger-watching there, scrambling
down the bank, past a stinking heap of wool,
to stake out the sett as the sky blackened
until we couldn't see a thing, only I knew
the rustling was the dead sheep walking.

Solstice

At 10, the centre spits out its citrus-coated late shift.
The solstice will occur in 23 minutes.

You zigzag the grid of the industrial estate,
its grey roads named for the species it ousted.

In Kestrel Way, two lorries are parked up. End to end
like copulating foxes. You glimpse discreet exchanges.

Faint beyond street lights, a little offset, the belt of Orion
is 3 in a row on a suspect fruit machine.

The solstice will occur in 9 minutes.
You see the system as grapes, tangerines, grapefruits,
    tilted, spinning.

A man wets the wheel of his truck,
spits the pips of alien words into the gutter.

Your online almanac has nailed the moment of this
    year's,
next year's ephemera, and it feels so good to have

the certainty of knowing when events will happen.
The solstice will occur in 1 minute.

That peardrop seen from the station, the swelling low
   pale star,
is your train, oncoming through the dark, 1 minute late.

Spawn

Tramping through damp grass, I trod
on this squashy mass of raw sprogs
dropped wrong, far from water. I scooped up
the lot, cupped in both hands a world
of black-cored worlds, some eyes white-blind
already, as dead as those would get
that spilled between wet fingers. I found
a fieldside pond fringed with bog, set
the glop in it like an offering.
My skin slime-blessed, I felt smug
at my small life-gift, and forgot
my part in the draining of the swamp,
the harrowing of earth, non-stop.

Stars

Emerging from the tent at 3am,
you see this field of fools, that hedge, the sea,
all subtly lit by an array of stars
in numbers that your mind cannot compute.
They're barnacles fixed on a dark flat rock,
and that faint streak of quartz marks other stars
too far to be distinguished one from one.
Each is a point, a dot of no dimension,
a chalk stab on a blackboard crammed with maths,
and still your brain insists that this big world
of fires and ice, its loves and hopes and lies,
its trillions of lives in millions
of forms would, in the heart of any star,
be in an instant crisped to kingdom come.

Tachyglossus

He will find her, however long it takes.
He tramps over the exotic scrubby grassland.
He's doing a television documentary.
He has a gismo that detects radio signals.

She's hiding in a hole that she has dug.
She's curled herself into a ball.
She's spiny with a beaklike nose and powerful digging
 claws.
She's been fitted with a radio transmitter.

He pinpoints the spot where she must be.
He yanks her out of her sanctuary.
He's adding to the sum of human knowledge.

She's a mess of earth and prickles.
She doesn't like what is happening to her.
She doesn't know about the sum of human knowledge.

Temple Meads

Beneath vast curves of brick and iron and stone,
I bend towards the small black tablet,
trying to establish a connection.

His works are mighty; the fabled bridge
that spans nothing, the great ship that came home.
Now, everything is shrunk. I search for links.

On an old map it's shown as simple fields.
There'll be some story of gods and nature
that a few clicks will find. My finger's poised.

The Badger

The badger came barrelling
in through the undergrowth,
bearing its snout like the
cone of a missile,
tearing the package
of spitpaper hexagons,
shrugging off stings from
the uniformed guardians,
grabbing the capsules of
tiny pale aliens.

This was deduced from
the scatter of brushwood,
the trample of grass, and
the relics of waspbabies
strewn as if spilt from
a split bag of bonbons.

This

Pub garden at low water. In the sun,
a frieze of teal and mallard, egret, swan,
first blue, first white-and-orange butterfly.
A snake has pulled its self out of the river.

It glistens, it's a rope of mud behind
the small hard head, the black and yellow collar.
It's printing a broad ess of shallow esses
into the fine brown slip-slope of the bank.

The camera stays unopened, blind, until
the snake is free and can't be seen for reeds.
The snake-marked mud, the intricate soft trace
will soon be tide-wiped. Then there'll just be this.

Two Leaves

Autumn has all boiled down to this; two leaves
from a plane tree have died and come to earth
to form this pavement tableau, hands the hue
of caramel with soft star-pointy fingers.

One, in an act of auto-origami,
has made itself a parcel of thin air,
enclosed a volume, has my mind convinced
for seconds of some solid frogginess.

The other one has wrapped its paper self
around the bottom of a plastic drainpipe
and stayed, gripped by the glue of its own damp,
some time-caught prey that tried, but failed, to flee.

Wormcasts

Among the crabshells and smashed granite,
a piece of seaglass, green as weed,
edges all pebbled away.

Footprints are longer-lasting
than the hailstones
that lodge in every hollowed heel.

Wormcasts. Imagine each real being
snug in its bunker
of cold wet sand.

MOLLUSCS

Dissolve

The snail has drawn its trail, unthinkingly,
across stone traces of its long-lost kin.
All forms evolve.

That reach of ours, to dive the depths of time,
to grasp the breadths, life as a billion riddles
for us to solve;

the best of what we are, the naming, knowing,
while in the warming oceans, all the shells
start to dissolve.

Malacophagy

In a pub that overlooked saltwater,
I ate a heap of mussels,
so sweet, so soft, I never tasted better,
well worth the mess and hassle.

On the beach at Sidmouth, one damp summer,
I chewed into a whelk,
a plug of solid snot or slimy rubber
not fit for decent folk.

In a big marquee one time, in public,
I went down on an oyster.
The sea was rising, falling in my gullet
for what seemed ever after.

By the Med, with chips, I chomped on suckers
of deep-fried octopus.
I fear my smart and subtle distant cousin
was hardly well-served thus.

The Slug and the Puffball

An ink-black slug
has fastened its soft face
to the paper-white body
of a small uprooted puffball.

The rasps
of its unseen toothed tongue
rock the puffball back and forth,
a motion that's almost
impossible to see,
but not quite.

Slugs

A day of rain has drawn them to the tarmac.
They have no dignity. Unhoused and naked,
holes and knobbed stalks on show, exuding mucus,

they feed on what's already rotted soft,
or on the foulest leavings of the dogs,
or on the innards of their gut-burst brothers.

They're thumb-thick felt-tip pens in black, soft grey
or subtle beige, though all the marks they make
are broad free-flowing lines of shiny silver.

Now one has raised its head and half its body
up from the mucky ground, a shallow 's'.
It looks as noble as a striking cobra.

Helix

Hodmandod, oddman, dodman with a packload,
backsacked pedlar down a shadowed back road,

hornywink, stalk-mounted periscope cameras,
headsticks unblinking, looking round corners,

snarlygig, gnarly fibonacci helter-skelter,
curly-pearly, slidy-spiral hardshelly shelter,

wallfish, furtive pub food on a limestone plateau,
dished up all scrumpied on a herb-wild butter platter.

Snails

The bonbon snails with their candy-curl shells
have claimed the plot in my absence.
They have inched skywards to higher than me.
One, lemon-yellow, has free-climbed the apple tree.
Another, with a swirl of dark chocolate,
has reached the peak of the highest beanpole.

They have been rasping at
the ripest autumn raspberries,
leaving them glistening with a thin glaze.
I swallow my distaste and eat the fruit.

Cepaea

To appear like candy, a sheen of pale lemon yellow,
a brittle swirl concealing your soft centre,

to carry your home as a fixed part of you,
to know that liberation, or that burden,

to look through eyes that softly telescope out,
then back into the sticky mush of you,

to be a mucus-machine, to keep on leaving
so much of your self behind wherever you crawl,

to shrink into the deep coils of your being,
to feel secure right up to the boot-crunch, bird-strike.

Snail

The snail lives in a shelter, hard and whorled
and watertight, which, when life gets too wild,
and round the universe it's hurled and whirled,
gets cracked and broken. Then the snail, unwilled,
instinctively, works with a slow, cold weld
to mend the damage to its one small world.

Polymath

The snail as geographer,
plotting the landforms of the garden,
the zones of vegetation, the cliffs and canyons.

The snail as physicist,
sticking to the undersides of the high leaves,
testing its adhesion against the force of gravity.

The snail as chemist,
combining ions of calcium and of carbonate
within the vessel of itself.

The snail as mathematician,
constructing with soft instruments,
in slow time, its logarithmic spiral.

Shell

Much like some mollusc alchemist,
secreting subtle matter from
the mantle of my mind,

I've built this twisted artefact,
this intricate fine-textured shell
for me to hide behind.

Light

Down in the rockpools,
the snakelocks and beadlets
and limpets hold tight.

Crunch of the barnacles
under your sandals.
You try to live right,

but dislodge the dogwhelks,
unanchor the mussels.
It's hard to walk light.

Mytilus

To capture them in pastels,
you'd need the smoky blue-grey shade
you'd use for the hazed hills
beyond the bay.

They're a smudged contour line,
a smear on the rocks,
a packed megalopolis
of a million times one.

To pick for the pot
this one, not this one,
to yank from its anchor
that one, and not its neighbour;

would that make you a little
like something majuscule,
like Death or Destiny
or God?

Holdfast

The kelp must glue its holdfast to the rock
to keep its stipe and bladed fronds secure,
as, should it fasten to a mussel shell,
then, with the roll of waves, its weighty pull
will snap the threads that hold the mussel tight,
and dash them both to pieces on the shore.

Nacre

'Hexagonal platelets
of aragonite...
arranged in a
continuous
parallel lamina.'

A boundless evening sky,
rain on the way,
thin cloud, the colours
coming through,
palest pink,
silver-blue.

The first stanza is taken from the Wikipedia entry for 'Nacre'.

Ming

Year after year, its dark hard shell
continued, thin line by line, to grow,
to increase by increments, to swell
so slow, so slow.

Pulled from its soft cold northern bed,
it's been, all the scientists now agree,
alive since the fifteenth century.
It's now stone dead.

Janthina

Janthina, Janthina,
far out on the ocean
in only your elegant
thin violet coat.

Janthina, Janthina,
with nothing but dribbles
of spittle and bubbles
to keep you afloat.

Janthina, Janthina,
blown hither and thither,
a thousand full fathoms
above the abyss,

and seizing the hearts of
the by-the-wind-sailors,
and rasping them ragged
with each savage kiss.

Ammonites

Jurassic seabeds have been lifted high,
and rocks are stuffed with child-delighting ammonites;
the scattered fragments of ribbed, grey rainbows,
those pale, frail whorls flattened to two dimensions,
the knobby giants in boulders on the shore,
and, best of all, these tiny, shiny trophies,
detailed and dense like diecast metal spirals.

But might we take them all away, and leave
the beach barren and fossil-less? No fear.
The kraken sea, with its billion suckers,
pulls Dorset back towards its jaws, bites hard
and bites again, spits out the endless relics.

Belemnites

Jumbles of points and hard arced edges
emerge from the mudstone of memory;
fragments of darts or of javelins,
snapped tips and shafts, broken bullets

of rock, nosecones from something ballistic,
a battlefield from the deep Jurassic
to be foraged from bleak wet beaches,
boxed and forgotten for fifty years

of getting the whole thing front-to-back.
These bonestones were arseward balances,
via phragmocones of aragonite,
to the squishy, squiddish business end.

Cameroceras

Out of a monster seashell, like a whorled
fallen steeple a yard across,
as long as a room,

emerge the tentacles. How many tentacles?
Cameroceras, the Chambered Horn,
crawls across the Ordovician seabed,

stalks and ambushes its smaller cousins.
They're gripped by tentacles (How many tentacles?)
and pulled towards the beak, the buccal mass,

and crushed, and smashed, and sucked.
Then Cameroceras crawls on and on,
into the Silurian. Into your head.

Nautilus

Displayed in a shop window
on a busy street

is this immortal coil, this masterpiece
of mathematical perfection.

It's like some fine pearly-cream ceramic,
expertly brush-stroked with bars of burnt sienna,

an elegant, opulent grand design,
a many-chambered mansion,

a plump volume of utterly reliable memoirs,
an epic poem composed in calcium carbonate.

Its tentacled denizen has long since
withered away. Maybe worse things happen,

afterwards, than for your life's work,
your magnum opus, to be forever

displayed in a shop window
on a busy street.

Argonaut

Small paper nautilus,
cockleshell octopus,
two of her tentacles
soft wands for conjuring
calcium carbonate
into her miracle
shell, light and delicate,
white ribbed and tuberculed
elegant watercraft,
henceforth and constantly
hers for the captaincy.

Benthic

They drift, any which way,
in ocean currents. Planktonic. All they know
to do is stay above the lightless abyss.

He's rootless, at the whim of others. Random.
Stuck in doldrums, then swept away in a stream
of traffic; M5, M6, M74.

It squats in its den. Benthic. It's built
a rough stone wall to hide itself behind.
It's scattered the empties of crabs, of clams.

He sits, camouflaged against
the armchair. So low. Soft fingertips
tickle the keys of his laptop.

Suckers

Stuck to the tank's thick wall, she's still, obscure
behind an outsized photograph of her,

then an arm curls, unfurls a double row
of suckers. You're amazed how fine they go.

The tip twists on itself, starts to explore
the apparatus up towards her core,

and disappears between her fattest suckers.
Her mantle, velvet-smooth before, now puckers.

You fancy that you see her colours change,
as pigment cells begin to rearrange,

but maybe that's all in your well-read mind.
'It's like my ball sack,' someone quips behind.

A line between your eye and hers might pass,
quick, laserlike, right through that toughened glass.

Escapologist

The octopus
explores her tank,
probes a loophole,
a gap between top and lid
no bigger than her horny beak
and, arm after suckered arm,
somehow oozes,
s
q
u
e
e
z
e
s
her whole pulpy self through,
plops onto the floor,
and lollops towards the open sea.

Pseudomorph

If an octopus's quick tattoos
fail to bamboozle or confuse
its enemies, it evades all trouble
by spurting a dark cloud, a liquid double,
a decoy, by inking a whole false body,
a volume of untrue autobiography.

Aliens

They are the closest thing to aliens
in all the world, so other, so grotesque,

although their eyes are, broadly, quite like ours,
a fine case of convergent evolution.

Their skin is smooth, unchanging, save for when
revealing some unknowable emotion.

Their sense of taste is rudimentary,
restricted to their strange unrasping tongue.

Their limbs are oddly few, quite suckerless.
Their sexual parts are where their mouths should be.

We cannot know what it is like to be one.
Their weird internal frame of beak-hard bone

means, though they're bright, they can be safely caged
where gaps are even bigger than their heads.

Octopus

We've climbed right to this tree-denuded peak,
and stand beneath the gases of the sky
as winners of the longest, toughest race,
wise presidents of everything we spy,

while on some seamount in the nurdled sea,
the highest, wisest of our bonefree kin
is watching out with fine convergent eye
and flashing warnings on its fast-change skin.

ACKNOWLEDGEMENTS

Thanks to the editors of the following, where some of these poems first appeared: *And Other Poems, Antiphon, Atrium, The Broadsheet, The Cannon's Mouth, Clear Poetry, The Curlew, Diversifly* (Fair Acre Press), *Dreich, Envoi, Foxglove Journal, The High Window, Ink Sweat and Tears, The Interpreter's House, The Journal, Lighten Up Online, Littoral Magazine, London Grip, Magma, Marble, Molly Bloom, Morphrog, Nine Muses Poetry, Orbis, Picaroon Poetry, Play* (Paper Dart Press), *Poetry Salzburg Review, The Poetry Village, The Rialto, Riggwelter, Runcible Spoon, South, Spilling Cocoa Over Martin Amis, Until the Stars Burn Out, The Wee Book of Wee Poems 1* (Hybriddreich), *Whirlagust* (Yaffle), *Words for the Wild, Zoomorphic*. Thanks also to the judges of the following competitions: Barn Owl Trust Wildlife Words Poetry Competition, Dempsey and Windle National Poetry Day Competition, HappenStance Feeling Blank Competition, Lichfield Literature Festival Poetry Competition, Manning's Pit Poetry Competition, Norwich Writers' Circle Poetry Competition, Sentinel Literary Quarterly Poetry Competition, Shepton Mallet Snowdrop Festival Poetry Competition, Ver Poets Open Competition, Ware Poets Open Poetry Competition, Winchester Poetry Prize, York Literature Festival/YorkMix Poetry Competition. Finally, my special thanks to Simon Williams, without whose Poem a Day group many of these poems would have remained unwritten.

THE HIGH WINDOW

The following collections are also available from our website, where further information will be found: thehighwindowpress.com

A Slow Blues, New and Selected Poems by David Cooke
Angles & Visions by Anthony Costello
The Emigrant's Farewell by James W. Wood
Four American Poets edited by Anthony Costello
Dust by Bethany W. Pope
From Inside by Anthony Howell
The Edge of Seeing by John Duffy
End Phrase by Mario Susko
Bloody, proud and murderous men, adulterers and enemies of God
by Steve Ely
Bare Bones by Norton Hodges
Wounded Light by James Russell
Bone Antler Stone by Tim Miller
Wardrobe Blues for a Japanese Lady by Alan Price
Trodden Before by Patricia McCarthy
Janky Tuk Tuks by Wendy Holborow
Cradle of Bones by Frances Sackett
Of Course, the Yellow Cab by Ken Champion
Forms of Exile: Selected Poems of Marina Tsvetaeva
translated by Belinda Cooke
West South North North South East by Daniel Bennett
Surfaces by Michael Lesher
Man Walking on Water with Tie Askew
by Margaret Wilmott
Songs of Realisation by Anthony Howell
Building a Kingdom, New and Selected Poems 1989-2019
by James W. Wood

The Unmaking by Tim O'Leary
Out of the Blue, Selected Poems by Wendy Klein
Daylight of Seagulls by Alice Allen
Man at the Ice House by Alison Mace
Empire of Eden by Tom Laichas
Visiting Hours by Kitty Coles
Is Anyone There? by Martin Zarrop
The Trio Confessions by Alan Price
Before Silence, a year's haiku by Michel Onfray
translated by Helen May Williams
Stem by Belinda Cooke
Slippage, Poems 2013-2018
By David Cooke
Walking Away, New and Selected Poems
by Shaun Traynor
The Leading Question by Roger Elkin
The Boycott by Sally Michaelson

Printed in Great Britain
by Amazon